GROWING UP

Visiting the Dentist

Charlotte Guillain

Heinemann Library
Chicago, Illinois

www.heinemannraintree.com
Visit our website to find out
more information about
Heinemann-Raintree books.

To order:

☎ Phone 888-454-2279

💻 Visit www.heinemannraintree.com
to browse our catalog and order online.

Edited by Dan Nunn, Rebecca Rissman, and Sian Smith
Designed by Joanna Hinton-Malivoire
Picture research by Elizabeth Alexander
Originated by Capstone Global Library Ltd
Printed in the United States of America by
  Worzalla Publishing.

15 14 13 12 11 10
10 9 8 7 6 5 4 3 2 1

Library of Congress Cataloging-in-Publication Data
Guillain, Charlotte.
  Visiting the dentist / Charlotte Guillain.
    p. cm. — (Growing up)
  Includes bibliographical references and index.
  ISBN 978-1-4329-4804-7 (hc) — ISBN 978-1-4329-4814-
6 (pb) 1. Children—Preparation for dental care—
Juvenile literature. 2. Dentistry—Juvenile literature. I. Title.
  RK63.G85 2011
  617.6—dc22   2010024198

Acknowledgments
We would like to thank the following for permission
to reproduce photographs: Alamy p. 19 (© Lisa
Eastman); Corbis pp. 5 (© Wolfgang Flamisch), 6 (©
Bill Varie/Somos Images), 7 (© Stefanie Grewel), 13
(© Paul Burns), 23 glossary receptionist (© Bill Varie/
Somos Images); Getty Images p. 8 (Indeed/Digital
Vision); iStockphoto p. 12 (© emre ogan); Photolibrary
pp. 4 (ERproductions Ltd/Blend Images), 15 (Image
Source), 16, 20 (Medicimage), 21 (UpperCut Images),
23 glossary tooth decay (Medicimage); Shutterstock
pp. 9 (© kristian sekulic), 10 (© Bork), 11 (© Bogac
Erguvenc), 14 (© Dmitriy Shironosov), 17 (© Jozsef
Szasz-Fabian), 18 (© Monkey Business Images), 23
glossary filling (© Jozsef Szasz-Fabian), 23 glossary
probe (© Bork), 23 glossary X-ray (© Bogac Erguvenc),
23 glossary fluoride (© Anton Prado photo).

Front cover photograph of a dentist and patient
reproduced with permission of Corbis (© Bill Varie/
Somos Images). Back cover photographs of a mirror
reproduced with permission of Shutterstock (©
Bork), and a mask reproduced with permission of
iStockphoto (© emre ogan).

We would like to thank Neesha Patel for her invaluable
help in the preparation of this book.

Every effort has been made to contact copyright
holders of material reproduced in this book. Any
omissions will be rectified in subsequent printings if
notice is given to the publisher.

Contents

Some words are shown in bold, **like this**.
You can find them in the glossary on page 23.

Why Do I Need to Go to the Dentist?

teeth

You need strong, healthy teeth to eat your food.

It is important to keep your teeth healthy.

You go to the dentist to check that your teeth are healthy and growing well.

The dentist can also help you if your teeth hurt or get knocked out.

What Happens When I Arrive?

When you get to the dentist's office, you will speak to the **receptionist**.

The receptionist will ask some questions, and there might be some forms to fill out.

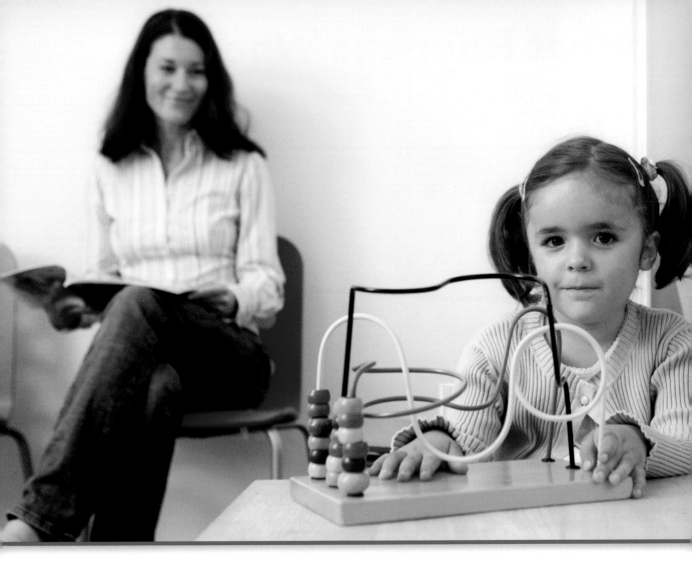

Then you sit quietly in the waiting room until the dentist is ready to see you.

There are often toys and books for you to play with and read.

What Happens When I Go In?

When you go into the dentist's room, the dentist or a dental assistant will meet you.

You might like to take your mom or dad into the room with you.

The dentist will ask you to sit in a special chair that moves up and down.

There is a big light over the chair to help the dentist see inside your mouth.

What Is the Dentist's Equipment For?

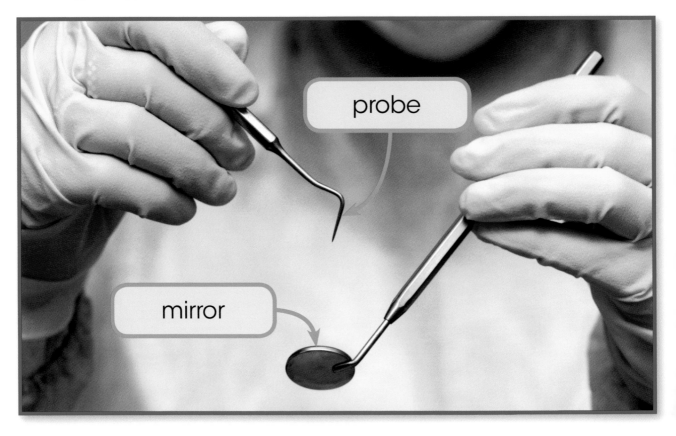

probe

mirror

The dentist uses a tool called a **probe** to look at your teeth.

The dentist uses a special mirror to see all around your teeth.

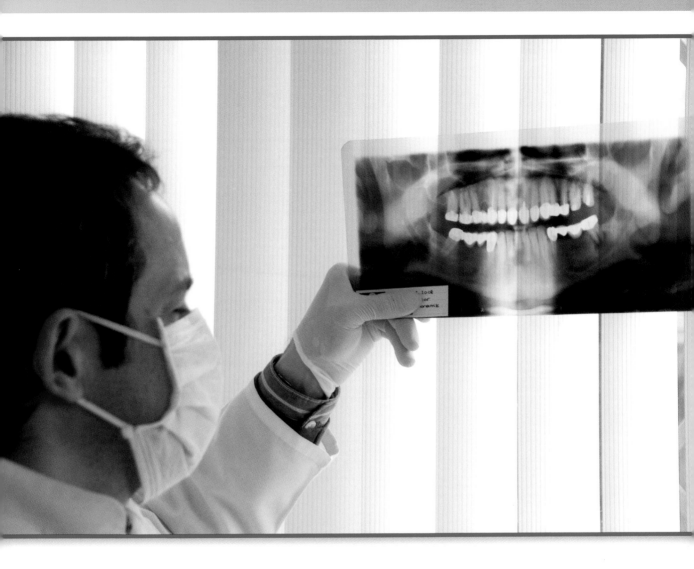

The dentist also has an **X-ray** machine.

This machine takes pictures that show the inside of your body.

Why Does the Dentist Wear a Mask and Gloves?

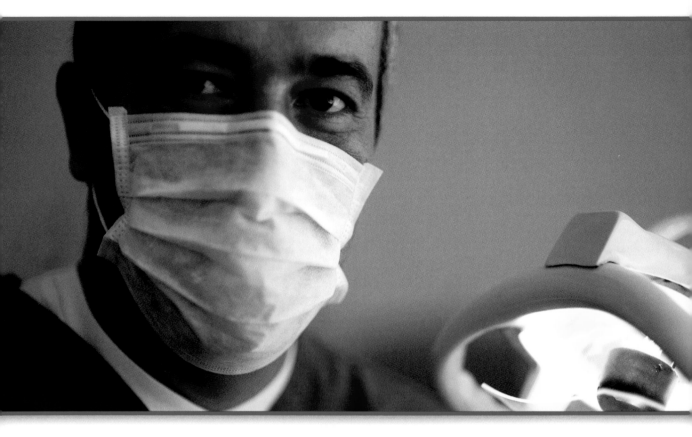

The dentist wears a mask over his or her nose and mouth.

The mask stops germs in the dentist's nose and mouth from spreading to you.

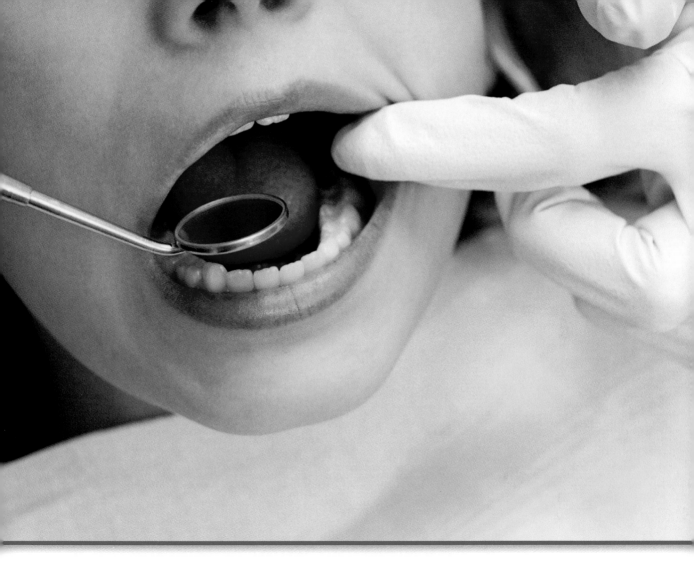

The dentist wears gloves when he or she touches your mouth.

This is to stop germs on the dentist's hands from spreading to you.

What Does the Dentist Need to Check?

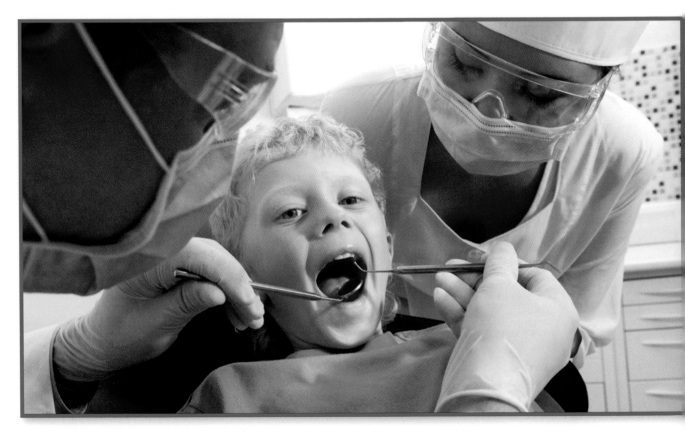

The dentist looks at your teeth to make sure they are healthy.

The dentist will use the mirror and **probe** to check your teeth.

The dentist will also count your teeth.

He or she might also give you advice on how to take care of your teeth.

What Happens If There Is a Problem?

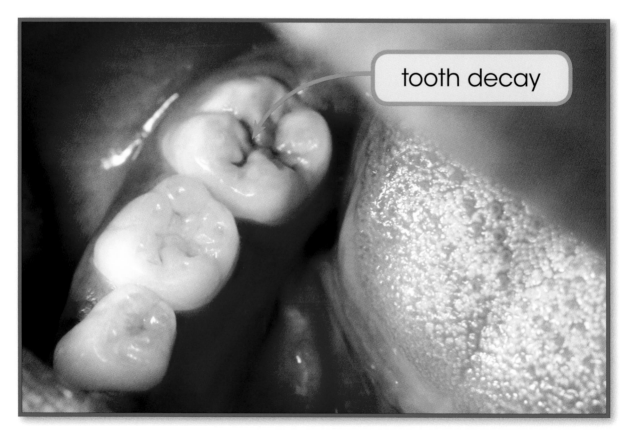

tooth decay

If you have a toothache, there might be a problem with your teeth.

Sometimes people get a toothache when they have **tooth decay**.

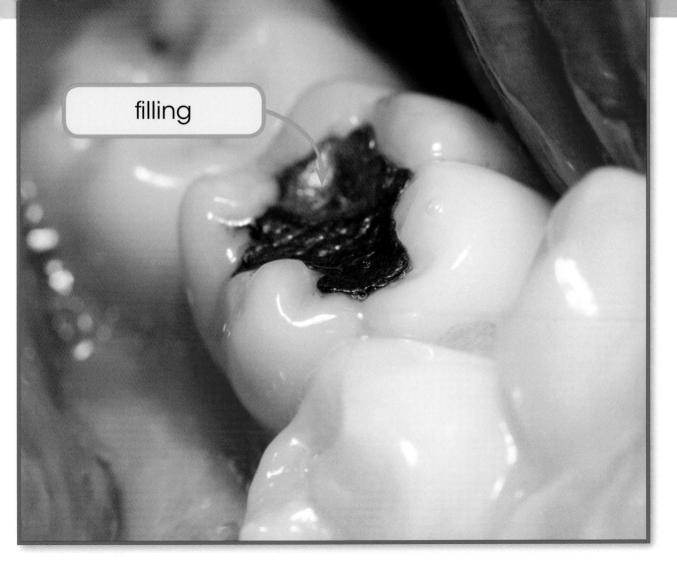

filling

If there is a hole in a tooth, the dentist may need to give you a **filling**.

A filling fills up the hole and stops the tooth from decaying any more.

Will Going to the Dentist Hurt?

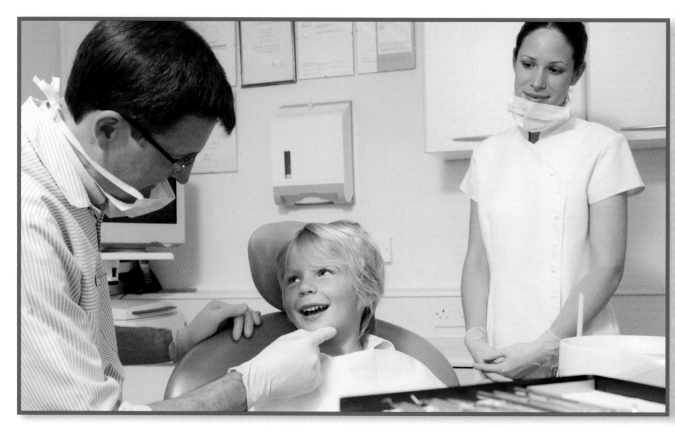

A normal checkup will not hurt at all.

It might just feel a little strange as the dentist looks around your mouth.

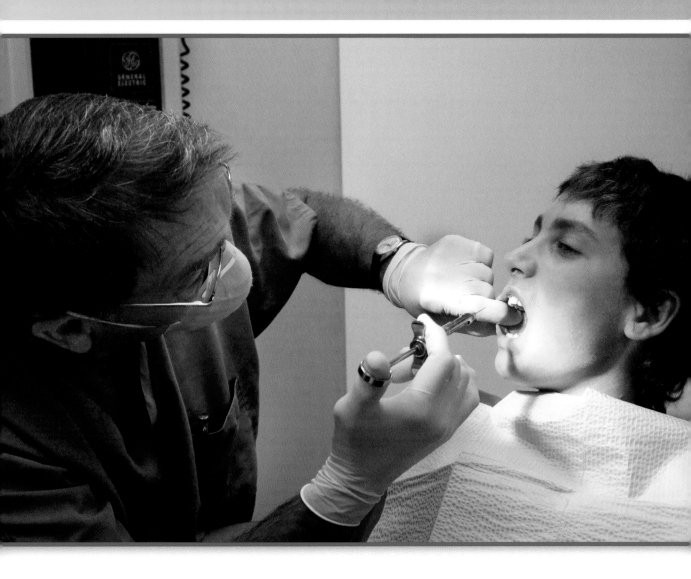

If you need a **filling**, the dentist might give you an injection.

This might prick a little, but it does not hurt for long.

What Happens at the End of a Checkup?

When the dentist has finished checking your teeth, you can rinse your mouth out.

You can spit the mouthwash out into a bowl by the chair.

The dentist might give you a sticker or a new toothbrush.

Your mom or dad might make your next appointment with the **receptionist**.

How to Care for Your Teeth

- Brush your teeth with **fluoride** toothpaste twice every day. Always brush your teeth before you go to bed.

- Try to drink milk or water. Too much fruit juice or soda can hurt your teeth.

- Don't eat too many sweets or other sugary foods.

- If you want a snack, have a piece of fruit.

- Milk and milk foods such as cheese help to make your teeth strong.

Picture Glossary

 **filling** material the dentist uses to fill a hole in a tooth

 **fluoride** chemical used in most toothpastes that helps to keep teeth healthy

 **probe** tool that dentists use to find out if teeth have holes

 **receptionist** person sitting at a desk near the entrance of a building, who meets people and tells them where to go

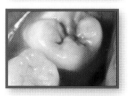 **tooth decay** damage and holes in teeth

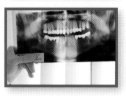 **X-ray** photograph of inside the body

Find Out More

Books

Civardi, Anna, and Stephen Cartwright. *Going to the Dentist* (First Experiences). Tulsa, Okla.: EDC, 2005.

Guillain, Charlotte. *Teeth* (Investigate). Chicago: Heinemann Library, 2009.

Royston, Angela. *Tooth Decay* (How's Your Health?). Mankato, Minn.: Black Rabbit, 2009.

Websites

Find out more information about taking care of your teeth:
http://kidshealth.org/kid/stay_healthy/body/teeth.html

Index